Skate-boarding Skills

by Jeff Hess

illustrated by Kevin Pedersen

A Creative GAMES PROJECTS and ACTIVITIES Book

Creative Education, Inc.
Mankato, Minnesota

Published by Creative Education, 123 South Broad Street, Mankato, Minnesota 56001.

Copyright © 1979 by Creative Education. International copyrights reserved in all countries. No part of this book may be reproduced in any form without written permission from the publisher. Printed in the United States.

Cover Illustration: Kevin Pedersen

Library of Congress Number: 79-15116   ISBN: 0-87191-672-X

Library of Congress Cataloging in Publication Data
Hess, Jeffrey A.   Skateboarding Skills.

SUMMARY: Presents a brief account of the renewed interest in skateboarding and describes a skateboard's various components. 1. Skateboarding—Juvenile literature. [1. Skateboarding. 2. Skateboards] I. Dahlstrom, Jon. II. Title.
GV859.8.H47   796.2'1   79-15116
ISBN 0-87191-672-X

TABLE OF CONTENTS

Señor Montalvo
and the Skateboard 5

The Birth (and Death)
of Skateboarding 7

The Man Who
Invented the Wheel 11

The Rebirth of
the Boards 13

Types of Skateboarding 14

Which Board Is Best? 17

About Safety 28

Learning the Basics 29

Beyond the Basics 32

SEÑOR MONTALVO
AND THE SKATEBOARD

About five hundred years ago in Spain there lived a writer named Garcia Ordoñez de Montalvo. Now, it is safe to say that Señor Montalvo knew little about skateboards. Certainly he never popped a nose wheelie or whirled into a 360°. Nevertheless, he seems to have accurately predicted where skateboarding would first make its appearance.

In one of his stories Montalvo described a strange and distant land where griffins lived in caves of gold. (A griffin, in case you happen to meet one, has the head and wings of an eagle and the body of a lion. It also has a bad temper and a big appetite.) Montalvo called this land "California." Although he was a little vague about how to get to California, he said it was located in the New World, not far from Paradise itself.

Soon after Montalvo published his story, the first Spanish explorers landed on what is now the west coast of the United States. These early conquistadors discovered neither gold nor griffins, and they certainly did not find the gates of Paradise. In spite of this, they named the newly discovered region California. Maybe it was their idea of a joke. In the long run, though, the joke was on them, for Montalvo's predictions gradually began to come true. After all, gold eventually <u>was</u> discovered in California. And Hollywood has let loose upon the world many beasts far stranger than griffins. As for Paradise — well, California <u>is</u> the birthplace of skateboarding. Just watch the face of any skateboarder as he leans low into a swooping, gravity-defying turn, and you'll see someone who's found Paradise.

THE BIRTH (AND DEATH) OF SKATEBOARDING

It all began in California in the early 1960s when surfing was the rage of the age. Wherever there were waves, surfers were riding them in. Unfortunately, there weren't always waves. Sometimes days would go by with hardly a ripple. During these lulls, surfers sat on the beach, grumbling at the ocean and wishing for a way to surf on dry land. Their wish came true.

No one knows exactly how it happened, but a group of surfers in southern California discovered that they could practice their surfing skills by balancing on a plank of wood nailed to roller skate wheels. When the ocean was being uncooperative, they rode on wheels instead of waves. With this discovery, "sidewalk surfing," or skateboarding, was born.

The first skateboards were crude, homemade affairs. The wooden tops tended to splinter and break; the wheels often wobbled and fell off. In 1962, however, a surf shop in North Hollywood, California began to make and sell more dependable models. Soon a number of companies were manufacturing skateboards.

In the beginning, skateboarding was simply a California curiosity, but after 1964 it quickly spread eastward to other parts of the country. By the summer of 1965, skateboarders seemed to be everywhere. You could find them tooling through the parking lots of Iowa, popping wheelies on the pavements of Pennsylvania, kick-turning in style down the sidewalks of New York. The newspapers called it a "national craze" and a "phenomenal fad." They compared the skateboard to the hula hoop, another California invention which had swept the nation in the late 1950s. And like the hula hoop, they predicted that this latest fad would soon die out.

The newspapers were right. In 1965, almost ten million skateboards were sold. But the next year, stores could hardly give them away. During 1966 people simply lost interest in skateboarding. Warehouses were filled with unsold and unwanted boards. Skateboard manufacturers called it "the Crash of '66."

Why did people so suddenly lose interest? What caused the death of skateboarding in the 1960s? No one knows for certain, but there seem to be at least two important reasons. First, skateboarding received a lot of bad publicity, and some of it was well deserved.

Perhaps because skateboarding was such a new sport, many people failed to realize that it could be a dangerous one. Some skateboarders insisted on riding through crowded sidewalks and busy streets, forcing many cities — from Providence, Rhode Island, to San Diego, California — to outlaw skateboarding as a "public nuisance" and a "traffic hazard." To make matters worse, few skateboarders bothered to wear safety equipment. The result was an epidemic of skateboarding injuries, causing many doctors to condemn the sport as "a new medical menace."

Although bad publicity contributed to the decline of skateboarding, the most important reason was probably basic defects in the skateboard itself. During the 1960s, many manufacturers made skateboard tops out of low grade wood, which frequently splintered. The wheels, however, were the biggest problem. At that time, all skateboards used a "composition" roller skate wheel which was basically made out of clay. Hard, fast, and smooth, these wheels were perfect for roller skating on indoor rinks. But skateboarding is an outdoor sport, and the clay wheels easily chipped and skidded on pavement. They simply could not provide the kind of gripping power, or traction, which is necessary for smooth, clean turns in skateboarding. The boards were so skittery that most riders could only master a few basic stunts. As a result, they soon grew tired of their "banana peels on wheels."

THE MAN WHO
INVENTED THE WHEEL

Anthropologists say nobody knows who invented the wheel. But skateboarders have the answer: the inventor of the wheel is Frank Nasworthy.

In 1970, eighteen-year-old Frank Nasworthy was a student at Virginia Polytechnic Institute. His college days, however, did not last very long. After joining a rather noisy political demonstration, Frank learned that he had been suspended from classes by the school. With unexpected free time on his hands, Frank took to hanging around a small plastics factory in Purcellville, Virginia, which was making roller skate wheels from a clear, amber-colored plastic called urethane. The wheels were not selling. Roller skaters disliked them because they were slower than clay wheels — urethane had too much gripping.

Now, Frank was not an expert on roller skating. His favorite sport was surfing, and like many surfers, he had also tried skateboarding. One day, out of curiosity, he decided to put urethane wheels on a skateboard. The results were astonishing. Instead of skidding and sliding through turns as he would do on clay wheels, the urethane hugged the pavement and kept right on rolling.

Excited by his discovery, Frank was convinced that urethane wheels could transform skateboarding into a completely new sport. At first no one listened. As far as manufacturers were concerned, skateboarding was dead. So Frank decided to go into business for himself.

THE REBIRTH
OF THE BOARDS

In 1973, after saving up some money by working in a restaurant, Frank moved to California and started his own company called "Cadillac Wheels." He began manufacturing skateboards with the new urethane wheels, and as a further improvement, he replaced the old wooden skateboard tops with flexible fiberglass, giving skateboarders even greater maneuverability and control.

The pattern of the 1960s began to repeat itself. Once again surfers in California were the first to ride the boards. And once again skateboarding quickly spread eastward. Except this time, it did not die out. With each year, skateboarding has continued to grow and grow, invading every part of the United States as well as Europe, Japan, and Australia. Frank Nasworth's wheels have made the difference. As Frank himself puts it, "Compared with the new skateboards, the old ones were like cars with wooden wheels. Skateboarding's a real sport now."

TYPES OF
SKATEBOARDING

Since its revival in the early 1970s, the skateboard has been put to a number of intriguing uses. Once again Californians have set the example — not always a good example. For instance, on August 3, 1975, two young men in Sepulveda, California used skateboards to make their getaway after robbing a doughnut shop. On a more constructive note, Emery Air Freight began hiring skateboarders in November, 1975, to deliver packages in downtown Los Angeles. Probably the most ambitious project was undertaken by three young men

from Morro Bay, California, who began skateboarding across the country on June 28, 1976. (By mid-July they had gotten as far as Minnesota.)

Although skateboarding will probably never become a major means of transportation, it is definitely going places as a sport. Each year an increasing number of skateboarding tournaments are being held throughout the United States. Generally, competition is offered in two main events: slalom and free style.

As in skiing, the slalom in skateboarding is a downhill racing event in which riders must weave through a series of markers. Sometimes the markers are arranged in a straight path ("in line" slalom), and sometimes they are laid out in a zigzag course ("switchback" slalom).

The free style competition is usually held on flat ground. Here the emphasis is not necessarily on speed, but on grace, strength, and ingenuity. Similar to free style ice skating or floor exercises in gymnastics, the contestants must put together their own program of board and body stunts, displaying creativity as well as skateboarding skill.

In addition to free style and slalom, some tournaments also offer a straight downhill racing event where speed is the only thing that matters. Since speed racing is very hazardous (skateboarders have been clocked at over fifty miles per hour), the downhill racing event is often restricted to professional skateboarding meets.

Of course, it is not necessary to compete in tournaments to have fun skateboarding. All you need is a stretch of open pavement and the wish to be wheeling. Skateboarding is also good exercise. As Dr. James Nicholas, physician for the New York Jets football team, has pointed out, "the boards are an excellent way to strengthen thigh, calf, and hip muscles."

WHICH BOARD IS BEST?

Skateboards come in a variety of sizes, shapes, and models, ranging in price from under $10 to over $50. Despite advertising claims, there is no special board which will magically suit everyone. The important thing is to find one that is right for you. In shopping for a skateboard, it is helpful to keep three things in mind:

(1) your own individual sense of balance and body size,

(2) the type of riding you're interested in doing,

(3) the amount of money you can afford to spend.

No matter what skateboard you look at, you'll find it composed of the same basic parts. All skateboards have a top (also called a "blank"), two pairs of wheels, and two trucks (the metal devices connecting the wheels to the blank). Since the quality of each of these parts affects the total performance of the board, it would be best to consider each separately.

WHEELS

Perhaps nothing affects overall performance as much as the wheels. The better the wheels, the smoother and safer the ride. Although all skateboard wheels are now made of urethane, some manufacturers use inferior grades of plastic. Unfortunately, unless you happen to be a plastics expert, it is almost impossible to tell the good stuff from the junk. It is therefore important either to shop at a store you can trust, or to buy established name brands which enjoy a good reputation among skateboarders.

Apart from urethane quality, the major differences among wheels are in bearings, size, and hardness.

Getting Your Bearings. Before talking about different types of wheel bearings, let's review how skateboard wheels work. A simple demonstration may help make things clear. First, find yourself a ring (a plain wedding band is good for this) and slip it snugly over one of your fingers. We'll call the finger an "axle" and the ring a "wheel." Now, try to spin the ring with the fingers of your other hand. Probably you'll find that it doesn't turn very smoothly. There's too much friction. (What you have here is a sticky wheel — not much good for skateboarding or anything else.)

One way to reduce friction is to coat your finger (the axle) with some kind of lubricant, like grease or oil. The problem with this method, however, is that

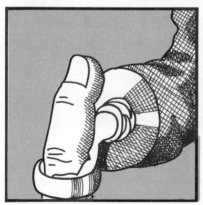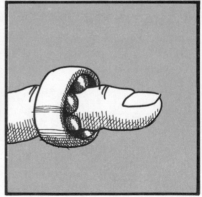

lubricants wear out and need to be replaced. For a longer-lasting method, find some beebees and slip about five of them between the ring and your finger. If you spin the ring now, you'll find that it rolls smoothly over the beebees, a device which lasts a long time.

Congratulations! You have just invented wheel bearings. Unfortunately, your invention is not yet perfect. You've probably noticed that the bearings have a nasty habit of falling out of the ring. There are a couple of ways to remedy this problem. One way is to cut a small groove around the inside of the wheel to house the bearings. Another way is to fit the bearings into a special ring of their own, which will allow them to turn freely without popping out of place. In both cases, the special track for the bearings is called a "race."

Skateboard wheels mainly use two types of bearings: "open bearings" and "sealed bearings." In the open bearing wheel, the bearings usually ride in groove-like races which have been molded into each side of the wheel. You can easily identify open bearing wheels because their ball bearings are clearly visible from the outside — you can see them nestled around the axle on both sides of the wheel. Although open bearing wheels work well at first, the exposed bearings gradually pick up dirt and begin to jam. Then it becomes necessary to take the wheel apart and clean the bearings, which can be a tricky business.

Wheels with sealed bearings, on the other hand, do not require any maintenance. In these wheels, the bearings are completely enclosed in ring-like races which protect them from dirt. Sealed bearings are also much quieter than open bearings — an important consideration in a sport where it helps to be able to hear cars creeping up behind you. The only disadvantage to sealed bearing wheels is their price. They are about twice as expensive as open bearing wheels.

Wheel Size. There are two helpful hints for selecting wheel size:

(1) the larger the diameter, the faster the speed;
(2) the greater the width, the better the traction.

Many skateboarders agree that a good, all-purpose wheel measures about two inches in width by two inches in diameter. This is sometimes called a "Stoker-size" wheel.

Wheel Hardness. If you poke a fingernail into the outer edge of different skateboard wheels, you'll see that some are softer than others. Usually, soft wheels have better traction and maneuverability than hard ones. They are also a bit slower. Their slowness, however, does not detract from their use in free style and slalom where they make up in cornering ability what they lack in speed. Only in straight speed racing do hard wheels deliver a clear advantage.

In checking wheels for hardness, it is best to do the fingernail test on both the inner and outer parts of the same wheel. Some wheels are made from two types of urethane: a softer outer layer wrapped around a hard inner core. As these wheels wear down, they become fast and slippery. Probably the best choice for an all-purpose wheel is one with fairly soft urethane and without a hard inner core.

Established Wheel Makers. Bennet, Cadillac, Power Paws, R.S.I. (Roller Sports, Inc.), Road Rider, Rolls Royce.

CHOOSING A BLANK

What Material? Perhaps no topic in skateboarding is more hotly debated than the question, "What is the best material for blanks?" Some riders favor hardwood blanks made from oak or ash, others prefer aluminum, and still others will only ride fiber glass. All three of these materials, however, make good, sturdy blanks. The main difference is in their degree of flexibility — hardwood has the least, fiber glass the most. Although it is possible to ride well on any of these blanks, beginners usually find that fiber glass is the easiest material to work with.

Good hardwood, aluminum, and fiber glass blanks are all expensive. If money is a problem, then you will probably have to settle for a plastic or plywood blank. Both of these materials work well enough in the beginning, but they tend to sag and lose their shape with repeated use, especially if the rider weighs more than 125 pounds.

No matter what type of blank you choose, make sure to put non-slip grip tape on its surface. The tape is absolutely necessary for good footing. Although there is now a special skateboard tape on the market, old-fashioned emery tape works just as well.

What Size Blank? Short blanks are the easiest to turn — and also to tip over. Long blanks have the best stability, especially at high speeds, but they are the most difficult to maneuver. If you're a stunt rider who does a lot of spinning and turning, you'll probably want a short board (about 24 inches). If, on the other hand, speed is your passion, it's definitely wisest to ride a long board (30 inches or longer) which won't wipe out half way down a hill. And if slalom is your specialty, look for an intermediate-size board (26 to 28 inches) which can deliver both speed and maneuverability.

But what if you're just beginning to skateboard and don't have a specialty? Then the important thing is to find a board on which you feel comfortable. There's an easy trick to help you make a decision.

First, place a yardstick on the floor, parallel to a wall. Now, facing the wall, put the toes of your hind foot on one end of the stick. (Which is your hind foot? Pick the one that feels more comfortable being in the back.) Bending your knees slightly, slide your front foot along the stick until you find a stance which allows you to rock in all directions without losing your balance. Comfortable? Good. Now, look down at the stick and measure the distance between your two feet, from small toe to small toe. If you add six inches to this measurement, you'll have the length of a good, all-purpose blank. For width, select a blank which is between 6 and 7 inches at its widest part.

What Shape Blank? The best blanks have smooth, flowing lines with blunt, rounded ends. It is wisest to stay away from sharp noses, pointy fins, or swallowtails. These so-called "streamlined" styles will not improve your skateboarding, and they definitely will not improve your looks if you fall on their sharp edges. One useful variation in shape, however, is the "kick tail" (or "nose tail," if it's in front). These slightly raised sections at the ends of the blank give riders increased leverage for doing tail and nose stunts like wheelies.

Established Blank Makers. Bahne, Banzai, Gordon and Smith, Hang Ten, Hobie, Hustler, Kanoa, R.S.I., X-Caliber, Zephyr.

TRUCKS

When you examine most skateboard trucks, you'll notice two rubber or urethane cushions on the main bolt of each truck. These cushions are shock absorbers. The bigger and springier they are, the smoother the ride. Some new skateboard models have steel springs instead of cushions.

The trucks also contain the steering mechanism of the skateboard. When you lean into a turn, your weight shifts from one side of the board to the other. This movement causes the pivot arms of the trucks to rotate in their sockets, guiding the wheels into the direction you're leaning.

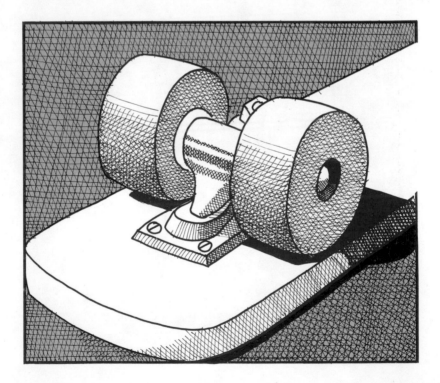

If your skateboard seems sluggish in turning, or if it turns too quickly, you can correct the problem by loosening or tightening the trucks. In either adjustment, it is first necessary to loosen the lock nut underneath the cushion cap by turning it several times in a clockwise direction with a wrench. To loosen the trucks, unscrew the main bolt by turning it with a screwdriver in a counter-clockwise direction. As you unscrew the bolt, the pivot arm and wheels become easier and easier to turn. If the wheels, however, are already too loose, then tighten up the trucks by screwing down the main bolt in a clockwise direction. At the end of either procedure, do not forget to tighten the lock nut snugly against the cushion cap. If you neglect to do this, the wheels might fall off while you're skateboarding.

Trucks are made out of brass, steel, or aluminum alloy. All of these materials are equally acceptable, as long as the workmanship is good. Make sure, though, that the hanger plates are attached to the blank by nuts and bolts, and not rivets. Hanger plates have a way of working loose. If they are bolted on, it is easy to tighten them up again. But if they are riveted to the blank, there is no way to fix them.

The length of truck axles ranges from about four to nine inches. The longer axles are more stable and are favored by slalom and speed racers.

Established Truck Makers. A.C.S. (American Cycle Systems), Bahne, Banzai, Bennet, Brewer, Chicago, R.S.I., Sure Grip, Tracker, X-Caliber.

ABOUT SAFETY

There are people who refuse to think about anything unpleasant. Sometimes they are called optimists. In skateboarding, however, they are mostly called stupid. Sooner or later, everyone wipes out, and it's only common sense to be prepared for it. By taking a few precautions, it's possible to keep skateboarding accidents and injuries to a minimum. Here are five basic rules for safe skateboarding:

(1) Do not skateboard on wet surfaces. Urethane loses its traction on water. No matter how good your wheels, they will skid like crazy on wet surfaces.

(2) Each time you skateboard, check out the area for sand, rocks, branches, and other obstacles that could send you sprawling.

(3) Wear safety padding. All types of skateboarding require gloves, elbow pads, and knee pads. If you're doing speed skating or upside down stunts like handstands, put on a helmet.

(4) Avoid busy streets and sidewalks.

(5) DO NOT EXCEED YOUR OWN LIMITS.

Different skateboarders have different capabilities. Only you know what you can or cannot do safely. If you're in doubt, then listen to your stomach. For example, if you're zipping down a hill and your stomach suddenly feels like you've swallowed a truck-load of frogs, SLOW DOWN. Your stomach is trying to tell you that you're being an idiot. And in Skateboarding there are no brave idiots — only damaged ones.

LEARNING THE BASICS

Skateboarding does not come naturally to most people. Don't be discouraged if at first you feel like a turkey trying to be a potato. Go slowly, and concentrate on learning the basics — things will improve with practice.

THE STANDARD POSITION

If you have never been on a skateboard before, it is a good idea to begin practicing on a soft surface, like grass or carpeting, where the wheels can't unexpectedly squirt out from under you. The first technique to master is "the standard position." Used by beginners and experts alike, this stance is the best all around position for balance and board control.

To assume the standard position, place your feet diagonally across the blank, with your front foot a little behind the front wheel, and your hind foot slightly ahead of the rear wheel. (Right-handed people usually like to ride with their left foot forward; "lefties" with their left foot in back.) Now, keeping your elbows tucked in at your waist, spread your arms slightly outward, and bend your knees a bit. Once you feel secure in the standard position, you are ready to take the board out on pavement and practice coasting.

COASTING

With the skateboard on level ground, place your front foot diagonally across the blank, slightly behind the front wheel. Now, slowly push off against the pavement with your hind foot. As the board begins to move, bring your hind foot onto the blank, and assume the standard position. Although it may be difficult at first, try to keep the center of your body over the center of the board. Any sudden body movements, frontwards or backwards, will spill you from the board. After you have mastered pushing off and coasting on flat ground, try your skill on a small, gentle hill.

TURNING

Turning on a skateboard is mostly a matter of leaning in the direction you want to go. To turn right, lean right; to turn left, lean left. As you lean into a turn, remember to keep your knees bent, your arms slightly spread, and your body tilted a bit forward. The important thing is to lean and not to twist. If you twist your body and shoulders around, you'll probably lose your balance and wipe out.

There are two ways to increase the sharpness of your turns:

(1) increase your lean,
(2) loosen the trucks (see section on TRUCKS).

As your turns become tighter and faster, you'll find it necessary to bend your knees more and more, until you're almost crouching on the board.

After you've learned to turn well in both directions, try zigzagging. The zigzag pattern is called "wedeling" in both skiing and skateboarding. Good practice for slalom, wedeling is also a method of cutting speed on a downhill run.

BEYOND THE BASICS

There are almost an endless number of stunts you can do on a skateboard. Some of them you'll probably invent for yourself. The following magazine and books may be of help in improving your skateboarding technique:

Skateboarder Magazine (12 issues a year for $12.00, Post Office Box 1028, Dana Point, California 92629).
Tom Cuthbertson, Anybody's Skateboard Book, Ten Speed Press.
Ben Davidson, The Skateboard Book, Grosset & Dunlap.
Jack Grant, Skateboarding, Celestial Arts.